in everything is
evidence of growth
in grace and a
thankful heart.

Charles Finney

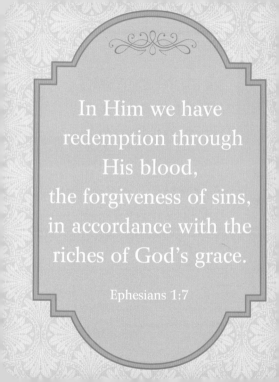

In Him we have
redemption through
His blood,
the forgiveness of sins,
in accordance with the
riches of God's grace.

Ephesians 1:7

The greater perfection
a soul aspires after,
the more dependent
it is upon divine grace.

Brother Lawrence

He gives us
grace and glory.
The LORD will
withhold no good thing
from those
who do what is right.

Psalm 84:11

Grace comes
into the soul,
as the morning sun
into the world; first a
dawning; then a light;
and at last the sun in
his full and excellent
brightness.

Thomas Adams

The LORD fulfills
the desires of those
who fear Him;
He hears their cry and
saves them.

Psalm 145:19

"My grace is sufficient for you, for My power is made perfect in weakness."

2 Corinthians 12:9

Grace keeps
us from worrying
because worry
deals with the past,
while grace deals
with the present
and future.

Joyce Meyer

The LORD is my
strength and shield.
I trust Him with all my
heart. He helps me,
and my heart
is filled with joy.

Psalm 28:7

Nothing
whatever pertaining
to godliness and
real holiness can
be accomplished
without grace.

St. Augustine

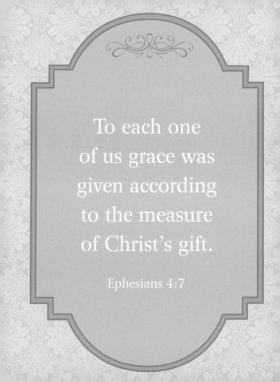

To each one
of us grace was
given according
to the measure
of Christ's gift.

Ephesians 4:7

Grace is the free,
undeserved
goodness and
favor of God to
mankind.

Matthew Henry

Grace and peace
be yours in
abundance.

2 Peter 1:2

Grace

Natural strength is
what we receive
from the hand
of God as Creator.
Spiritual strength
is what we receive
from God in grace.

Watchman Nee

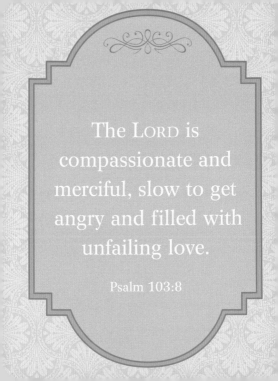

The LORD is compassionate and merciful, slow to get angry and filled with unfailing love.

Psalm 103:8

Never think that
you can live to God
by your own power;
always look to and
rely on Him for
assistance, for all
strength and grace.

David Brainerd

For it is by grace
you have been saved,
through faith – and this
is not from yourselves,
it is the gift of God.

Ephesians 2:8

Amid the
darkness of sin,
the light of God's
grace shines in.

Anonymous

Let us then approach God's throne of grace with confidence, so that we may receive mercy and find grace to help us in our time of need.

Hebrews 4:16

As grace
is first from God,
so it is continually
from Him, as much
as light is all day long
from the sun.

Jonathan Edwards

God is able
to make all grace
abound toward you,
that you, always having
all sufficiency in all
things, may have an
abundance for every
good work.

2 Corinthians 9:8

God doesn't
just give us grace,
He gives us Jesus,
the Lord of grace.

Joni Eareckson Tada

I trust in Your
unfailing love. I will
rejoice because You
have rescued me.
I will sing to the
LORD because He is
good to me.

Psalm 13:5-6

If you live close to God
and His infinite grace,
you don't have to tell;
it shows on your face.

Anonymous

If we walk in the light
as He is in the light,
we have fellowship
with one another,
and the blood of Jesus
cleanses us from all sin.

1 John 1:7

Grace is love
that cares
and stoops
and rescues.

John Stott

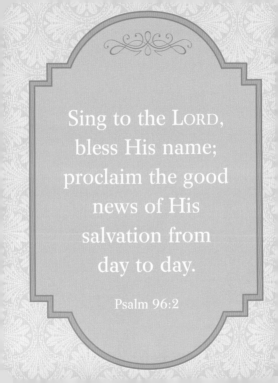

Sing to the LORD,
bless His name;
proclaim the good
news of His
salvation from
day to day.

Psalm 96:2

By grace I understand
the favor of God,
and also the gifts
of His Spirit in us;
love, kindness, patience,
obedience, mercifulness,
peace, concord,
and such like.

William Tyndale

Return to the
LORD your God,
for He is gracious
and compassionate,
slow to anger and
abounding in love.

Joel 2:13

Where the will
of God leads you,
the grace of God
will keep you.

Anonymous

Let us run with perseverance the race marked out for us, fixing our eyes on Jesus, the pioneer and perfecter of faith.

Hebrews 12:1-2

I am not what I ought to be. I am not what I hope to be. But still, I am not what I used to be. And by the grace of God, I am what I am.

John Newton

May our Lord
Jesus Christ Himself
and God our Father
encourage your hearts
and strengthen you
in every good deed
and word.

2 Thessalonians 2:16-17

Grace is something
you can never get
but can only be given.
There's no way
to earn it or deserve
it any more than
you can deserve
the taste of raspberries
and cream.

Frederick Buechner

From His abundance
we have all received
one gracious blessing
after another.

John 1:16

We believe that the work of regeneration, conversion, sanctification and faith, is not an act of man's free will, but of the mighty and irresistible grace of God.

Charles H. Spurgeon

May you experience the love of Christ, though it is too great to understand fully. Then you will be made complete with all the fullness of life.

Ephesians 3:19

Knowledge is but
folly unless it is
guided by grace.

George Herbert

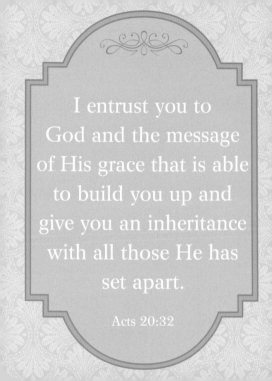

I entrust you to
God and the message
of His grace that is able
to build you up and
give you an inheritance
with all those He has
set apart.

Acts 20:32

Grace is but glory
begun, and glory is
but grace perfected.

Jonathan Edwards

Sin shall not
have dominion
over you, for you are
not under law but
under grace.

Romans 6:14

Faith is the
champion of grace,
and love the nurse;
but humility is the
beauty of grace.

Thomas Brooks

Through Him we have gained access by faith into this grace in which we now stand. And we boast in the hope of the glory of God.

Romans 5:2

Christ's death
to sin and His
satisfaction of God's
justice opened the
way for the reign of
grace in our lives.

Jerry Bridges

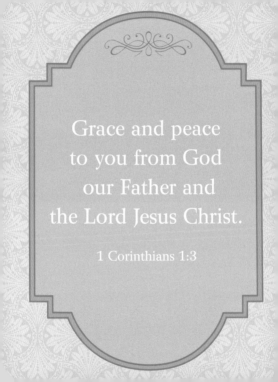

Grace and peace
to you from God
our Father and
the Lord Jesus Christ.

1 Corinthians 1:3

The law tells me
how crooked I am.
Grace comes
along and
straightens me out.

Dwight L. Moody

The grace of God
has been revealed,
bringing salvation
to all people.

Titus 2:11

Experiencing
God's grace
in our brokenness,
reminds us that His
love never fails.

Anonymous

The God of all grace, after you have suffered a little while, will Himself restore you and make you strong, firm and steadfast.

1 Peter 5:10

God did
not choose us
because we were
worthy, but by
choosing us He
makes us worthy.

Thomas Watson

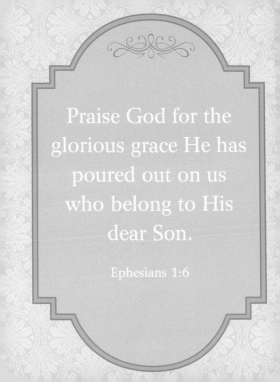

Praise God for the glorious grace He has poured out on us who belong to His dear Son.

Ephesians 1:6

He rides pleasantly
enough whom the
grace of God carries.

Thomas à Kempis

We are all saved
the same way,
by the undeserved
grace of the Lord Jesus.

Acts 15:11

To live by grace
is to live solely by the
merit of Jesus Christ.
To live by grace
is to base my entire
relationship with
God on my union
with Christ.

Jerry Bridges

You know the
generous grace of our
Lord Jesus Christ.
Though He was rich,
yet for your sakes He
became poor.

2 Corinthians 8:9

All Christian power
springs from
communion with
God and from the
indwelling
of divine grace.

James H. Aughey

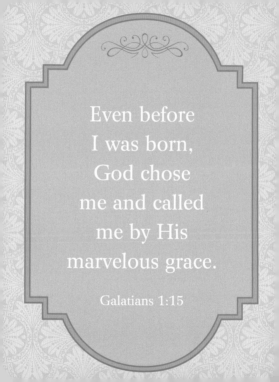

Even before
I was born,
God chose
me and called
me by His
marvelous grace.

Galatians 1:15

Grace means
undeserved kindness.
It is the gift of God to
man the moment he
sees he is unworthy
of God's favor.

Dwight L. Moody

Because of His
grace He declared
us righteous and gave
us confidence that we
will inherit eternal life.

Titus 3:7

The Word provides
a mental depository
for the Holy Spirit
to use to mediate
His grace to us,
whatever our need for
grace might be.

Jerry Bridges

Look after each
other so that none
of you fails to receive
the grace of God.

Hebrews 12:15

Grace is not
an excuse for a
sloppy life, it's
the power to
overcome it!

Joyce Meyer

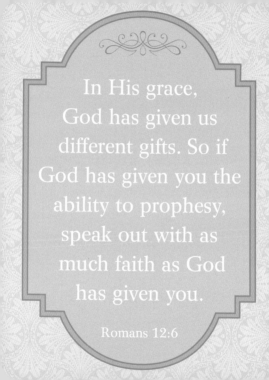

In His grace,
God has given us
different gifts. So if
God has given you the
ability to prophesy,
speak out with as
much faith as God
has given you.

Romans 12:6

God is an embodiment of hope and sympathy and He will never leave you in a precarious situation without providing you with hope and grace.

Kemmy Nola

The Lord be with
your spirit. Grace
be with you.

2 Timothy 4:22

God never leads
us where He cannot
keep us. His grace is
always sufficient for us
in any and every
circumstance of life.

Anonymous

The Lord is full
of tenderness
and mercy.

James 5:11

Grace is the very opposite of merit ... Grace is not only undeserved favor, but it is favor shown to the one who has deserved the very opposite.

Harry Ironside

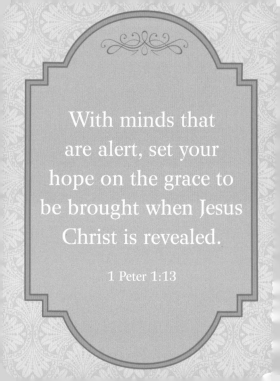

With minds that
are alert, set your
hope on the grace to
be brought when Jesus
Christ is revealed.

1 Peter 1:13

Grace means
the full and free
forgiveness of every
sin, without God
demanding or
expecting anything
from the one
so forgiven.

J. N. Darby

Grace be with all
those who love our
Lord Jesus Christ
in sincerity.

Ephesians 6:24

Even in my darkest hour
the Lord will bless
me with His power,
His loving grace
will sure abound,
in His sweet care
I shall be found.

Anonymous

To Him who loved
us and washed us from
our sins in His
own blood ... to
Him be glory and
dominion forever
and ever. Amen.

Revelation 1:5-6

Grace does away the distance between the sinner and God. Grace meets the sinner where he stands; grace approaches him just as he is.

Horatius Bonar

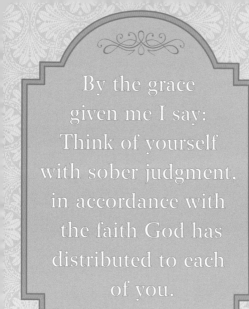

By the grace given me I say: Think of yourself with sober judgment, in accordance with the faith God has distributed to each of you.

Romans 12:3

Lord, please give
me the grace to be
content, the patience
to wait on Your timing,
and the faith to know
Your hand is always
on my heart.

Nishan Panwar

The Word became flesh and made His dwelling among us. We have seen His glory, the glory of the one and only Son, who came from the Father, full of grace and truth.

John 1:14

Every punishment
from God is pure
justice and every
blessing from Him
is pure grace.

Ritu Ghatourey

Do not withhold
Your tender mercies
from me, O LORD;
let Your lovingkindness
and Your truth
continually preserve me.

Psalm 40:11

The love and grace of God is within, but it's up to you to reveal it. An act of love and compassion is an example of God's grace.

Carniel Dunlop

Let us come boldly to the throne of our gracious God. There we will receive His mercy, and we will find grace to help us when we need it most.

Hebrews 4:16

When problems are
so big and your strength
is no longer enough,
don't give up! Because,
where your strength
ends, the grace of
God begins!

Anonymous

His merciful kindness
is great toward us,
and the truth of the
LORD endures forever.

Psalm 117:2

Grace expresses
two complementary
thoughts: God's
unmerited favor to us
through Christ, and God's
divine assistance to us
through the Holy Spirit.

Jerry Bridges

Let your speech always be with grace, seasoned with salt, that you may know how you ought to answer each one.

Colossians 4:6

Frustration,
complication,
and misery are
available in
abundance, but
so is God's grace.

Joyce Meyer

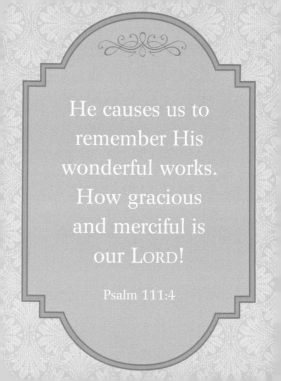

He causes us to
remember His
wonderful works.
How gracious
and merciful is
our LORD!

Psalm 111:4

Grace is not simply leniency when we have sinned. Grace is the enabling gift of God not to sin. Grace is power, not just pardon.

John Piper

Mercy, peace and love be yours in abundance.

Jude 2

Grace is not
the freedom to sin;
it is the power
to live a holy life.

Joyce Meyer

Since it is through
God's kindness, then it is
not by their good works.
For in that case,
God's grace would not be
what it really is – free and
undeserved.

Romans 11:6

© 2014 Christian Art Gifts, RSA
Christian Art Gifts Inc., IL, USA

Designed by Christian Art Gifts

Images used under license from Shutterstock.com

Scripture quotations are taken from the *Holy Bible*,
New International Version® NIV®. Copyright © 1973, 1978, 1984, 2011
by International Bible Society. Used by permission of Biblica, Inc.®.
All rights reserved worldwide.

Scripture quotations are taken from the *Holy Bible*,
New Living Translation®. Copyright © 1996, 2004, 2007
by Tyndale House Foundation. Used by permission of Tyndale House
Publishers, Inc.,Carol Stream, Illinois 60188.
All rights reserved.

Scripture quotations are taken from the New King James Version.
Copyright © 1979, 1980, 1982 by Thomas Nelson, Inc.
Used by permission. All rights reserved.

ISBN 978-1-4321-1254-7

Printed in China

TO:

FROM: